W9-CPE-832

How To Convince Your Parents You Can...

Care For A Wild Chincoteague Pony

Mary Boone

Mitchell Lane
PUBLISHERS

P.O. Box 196
Hockessin, Delaware 19707
Visit us on the web: www.mitchelllane.com
Comments? email us: mitchelllane@mitchelllane.com

NOV 2008

Mitchell Lane
PUBLISHERS

Printing   1   2   3   4   5   6   7   8   9

A Robbie Reader/How to Convince Your Parents You Can...

Care for a Pet Bunny   Care for a Pet Mouse
Care for a Pet Chameleon   Care for a Pet Snake
Care for a Pet Chimpanzee   Care for a Pet Tarantula
Care for a Pet Ferret   Care for a Potbellied Pig
Care for a Pet Horse   **Care for a Wild Chincoteague Pony**

Library of Congress Cataloging-in-Publication Data
Boone, Mary.
   Care for a wild chincoteague pony / by Mary Boone.
      p. cm. — (A Robbie Reader—How to convince your parents you can...)
   Includes bibliographical references and index.
   ISBN 978-1-58415-663-5 (library bound)
   1. Chincoteague pony—Juvenile literature. I. Title.
   SF315.2.C4B66 2008
   636.1'6—dc22
                                                                                    2008002247

ABOUT THE AUTHOR: Mary Boone grew up on a horse farm in northeast Iowa and attended her first wild horse and pony auction in 1982. She regrets she was never able to convince her parents to buy a wild pony. Mary now lives in Tacoma, Washington, and has written a dozen books for young readers. When she's not writing, she enjoys running, biking, and being outdoors with her husband, Mitch, and children, Eve and Eli.

PHOTO CREDITS: Cover, pp. 1, 3, 10, 29–32—Barbara Marvis; p. 4—Chincoteague Island.net; p. 8—Chincoteague Volunteer Fire Company; p. 12 (bottom), 15—Christopher Evanson/United States Coast Guard; p. 12 (top), 16, 17—Chincoteague and Assateague Islands and the Chincoteague Volunteer Fire Company; p. 14—Sharon Beck; pp. 18, 21—Robin Pool; pp. 22, 24—Lois Szymanski; p. 26—Barb Hull; p. 28—Tom Suddreth.

   Special thanks to Lois Szymanski of Feather Fund and Adrienne Wolfe of Rolling Bay Farm Chincoteague Ponies/Chincoteague Pony Breeders Association for their help with this book.

TABLE OF CONTENTS

Words in **bold** type can be found in the glossary.

Chincoteague ponies are beautiful animals. Their extra-thick manes and tails can grow to great lengths if allowed.

WILD ABOUT WILD PONIES

Stand perfectly still and imagine this: You're on a small island off the coast of Virginia and you think you're alone. Suddenly a herd of ponies comes galloping down the beach. *Thrump, thrump, thrump*—their hooves beat the sand as they get closer. Their manes fly and their nostrils flare. Like other ponies, these are strong and graceful. Unlike other ponies, these are wild.

In a nation filled with skyscrapers and cement, it's hard to believe that herds of wild ponies still exist in the United States, but they do. About three hundred wild ponies live on Assateague (AS-uh-teeg) Island.

Many people first learned about these famous wild ponies from a book called *Misty of Chincoteague* (SHING-koh-teeg) by Marguerite Henry. The story was written in 1947. The book is fictional, but it is based on real people, real ponies, and a real place. Chincoteague Island is tucked between windy and wild Assateague and the coast of Virginia.

Assateague is only a mile wide, but thirty-seven miles long. The invisible border between Maryland and Virginia stretches over the water and across the island. Two groups of ponies live on the island; a fence in the middle of the island keeps them apart. The herd on the Maryland side is owned and managed by the National Park Service. The Virginia herd is owned by the Chincoteague, Virginia, fire department. The animals in the Virginia herd are often referred to as Chincoteague ponies.

Anyone can visit either group of wild ponies. What you may not know is that you can buy one of these ponies to care for and keep as a pet of your own.

Owning a wild pony is a lot like owning any other pony. Ponies need daily care and exercise. You can ride your pony in races, shows, or just for fun. Ponies can be trained to pull carts or wagons. If you live on a farm, you can put your pony to work helping to round up cattle or sheep. Ponies are good learners. With patience and practice, you can teach your pony to respond to your requests and do basic tricks.

Riding a pony is good exercise. It gets you outdoors in the fresh air and gives you an exciting way to enjoy nature. If you've never ridden a pony before, you'll quickly learn it takes balance and leg strength to stay in the saddle while **trotting** (TRAH-ting) across a rough field. Riding will help improve your balance.

funFACTS

Ponies are herd animals. They live in groups and help each other survive threats from the weather and other creatures.

Do any of your friends have ponies? Riding with them is a great way to add to the fun. You might also want to take lessons together or join a club, like a U.S. Pony Club or 4-H, where you can learn more about riding and caring for horses.

Above all, ponies make great companions. Your pony will become a friend who looks forward to spending time with you. When you enter the barn, your pony will likely whinny a greeting to you.

Do you think you might want to have a wild pony of your own? If so, you'll want to read the rest of this book to learn all about these amazing animals.

Ponies run wild on Assateague Island. Visitors can go right onto the beaches where the animals roam, but they should never feed them.

 **Chapter Two** 2

FROM TAME TO WILD

The wild ponies on Assateague Island are feral (FAYR-ul), which means they are the **descendants** (dee-SEN-dents) of tame animals that were released into the wild.

Some people believe the ponies swam to Assateague from a shipwrecked Spanish **galleon** (GAL-ee-on). Scientists have not found any proof that this is true. It is more likely that horses were brought to Assateague in the late 1600s by mainland farmers who didn't want to build fences for their animals or pay taxes on them.

Not all wild horses and ponies live on Assateague Island. Wild ponies also live on islands off the coasts of North Carolina, Georgia, and Nova Scotia in Canada. About 30,000 wild horses roam through Arizona, Colorado, Idaho, Montana, Nevada, New Mexico, North Dakota, Oregon, Utah, and Wyoming.

Wild ponies graze outside a restaurant on Chincoteague. Many people on Chincoteague purchase the ponies from the fire department and keep them on their property.

Assateague ponies stand 12 to 13 hands tall. A hand equals four inches. Horses and ponies are measured from the ground to the withers, the highest point of the shoulders. A horse is taller than 14 hands, 2 inches. A pony is that size or smaller.

Assateague ponies come in a variety of colors. Many of the ponies are "pinto," with splotches of color that are shaped like pieces from a very big jigsaw puzzle.

Besides size, horses and ponies look different. Ponies usually have thicker coats, shorter legs, thicker necks, and broader foreheads.

Assateague ponies may have descended from horses, but now, after many years of eating only marsh grasses and twigs, they are more like ponies. Because the grasses they eat grow in saltwater, the ponies drink about twice as much water as tame ponies. All that water, combined with a high-salt diet,

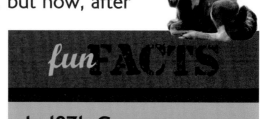

funFACTS

In 1971, Congress passed a law protecting wild horses, ponies, and burros in the United States. It is called the Wild Free-Roaming Horses and Burros Act.

makes their stomachs swell. Many people mistakenly think the round-bellied ponies are pregnant.

Wild ponies are hardy animals. They are tough enough to survive bug bites, extreme heat, and storms with violent winds. Many of the ponies live in the island's marshes, close to the grasses they eat. **Foals** (FOHLS) are usually born in late spring and live with their mothers in a family group called a band. Each band is usually made up of two to ten **mares** (MAYRS), their foals, and a **stallion** (STAAL-yen).

Horses and ponies can be wonderful, loving companions, but if you get one, you need to plan on caring for it for many years. Wild ponies live 25 to 30 years. Some even live to be 40 years old.

Each July, Chincoteague firefighters round up the wild ponies.

At low tide, the "saltwater cowboys" swim the ponies from Assateague to Chincoteague Island.

THE WILD PONY AUCTION

If you decide you want to buy a wild pony, the Chincoteague Pony Auction is a good place to go. The auction often attracts as many as 40,000 horse and pony lovers.

The auction began in 1924. Except for 1944, it has been held each year since. On the last Wednesday of July, a group of Chincoteague firefighters and other volunteers become "saltwater cowboys." They ride their own horses through the water to Assateague Island and round up the Virginia herd of horses. The cowboys let the ponies rest on the beach until low tide. When the water is at its lowest point and currents are calm, the wild ponies are herded into Assateague Channel for the five-minute swim to Chincoteague Island.

As with most wild horse and pony auctions, the Chincoteague ponies are penned up the day before the sale so that people can decide which ones they

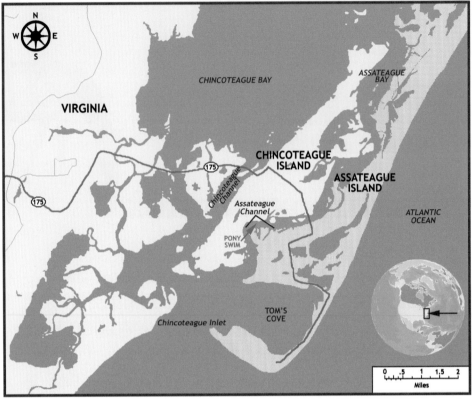

Chincoteague and Assateague islands are among a handful of barrier islands off the coast of Virginia and Maryland. In addition to horses, the islands and surrounding waters are home to dolphins and many migratory birds.

might want to bid on. The locals on Chincoteague Island call this "pony penning."

If you plan to buy a pony, you should arrive at the sale early to pick up a program and look over the ponies. Steer away from any with dull coats or sores. Avoid those that bite at themselves, other ponies, or people. Don't buy a pony that limps. By watching the ponies for a while, you'll begin to see which ones are

Thousands of tourists, some standing waist-deep in water, wait hours to watch the annual pony swim. It takes less than five minutes for the herd to swim from Assateague to Chincoteague.

calm, which ones aren't afraid of people, and which ones are especially nervous. Make notes about the ponies you like best.

Auction day brings a flurry of activity. Bidders and those wanting to see the action arrive well ahead of the 8:00 A.M. start time. Ponies are brought into the outdoor sale ring one at a time. The

Once the ponies arrive on Chincoteague Island, they are penned so that visitors can get a good look. Don't those foals look exhausted?

auctioneer gives a start price for each pony. Then, talking so fast the words are sometimes hard to understand, the auctioneer shouts out higher and higher prices until no one in the crowd is willing to pay more. The pony is sold to the highest bidder— the person who is willing to pay the most. In 1924, fifteen foals were sold for $25 to $50 each. In 2007, seventy-three ponies were sold for an average cost of $2,442.

After the sale, the remaining herd swims back to Assateague. Some schools and individuals buy foals they don't keep. These sponsors have their

Foals are brought into the auction ring one at a time so that people can bid on them. In 2007, a record $17,500 was paid for one of the ponies.

pictures taken with their foals, then they let them swim with the herd back to Assateague.

The auction raises money for the Chincoteague Volunteer Fire Company, which cares for the Virginia herd. The auction helps control the number of ponies. Assateague is not large; if there were too many ponies in the herd, there wouldn't be enough food for all.

It's easy to get caught up in the excitement of the Chincoteague auction and the carnival that follows. Don't forget: Buying a wild pony is a commitment that will affect your whole family and change your life.

Summer Barrick's Starlight Blessing is one of nearly 2,000 privately owned Chincoteague ponies that live throughout the United States and Canada.

BIG RESPONSIBILITY

Owning any pony is a big responsibility. Owning a wild pony can be an even bigger responsibility.

Generally when you buy a pony, it has already been trained. Wild ponies have never worn a halter, bridle, or saddle. Training a wild pony will take extra work and help from an adult. In fact, you won't be able to own and care for a wild pony without help from an adult.

You'll need money to buy your pony and a trailer to get it home. All ponies purchased at the Chincoteague auction must be **registered** (REH-jis-terd), so you will need help filling out paperwork.

Once you're home, you will need a fenced pasture for your pony. You will need a stall in a barn that lets your pony get away from the rain, wind, cold, and heat. You will need straw or wood chips for bedding, and buckets for food and water.

Chincoteague ponies are known as "easy keepers," meaning they don't need a lot of fancy feed. A popular joke among owners is "a Chincoteague pony can get fat on a cement slab."

Your pony will eat grass and clover from its pasture, but you must also feed it hay and grain or packaged feed. A mineral or salt block should be placed in the stall for your pony to lick.

It's important to keep your pony's stall clean. You will need a pitchfork, shovel, and wheelbarrow to remove **manure** (meh-NOOR) and dirty bedding. You must clean your pony's stall every day.

You will need a halter and a lead rope for walking your pony. You will need a saddle and a bridle for riding. You may need a blanket for your pony to wear if it gets extremely cold where you live. You will need bug spray, combs, brushes, and a hoof pick to clean dirt and rocks out of your pony's hooves.

Your pony's hooves will need to be trimmed several times each year. They may even need to have metal shoes put on if you ride your pony a lot. A **farrier** (FAA-ree-ur) must be paid to trim and shoe your pony's feet.

If your pony gets sick or hurt, you'll need a **veterinarian** (veh-truh-NAYR-ee-un) to care for it. Your pony will also need regular checkups to help it stay healthy.

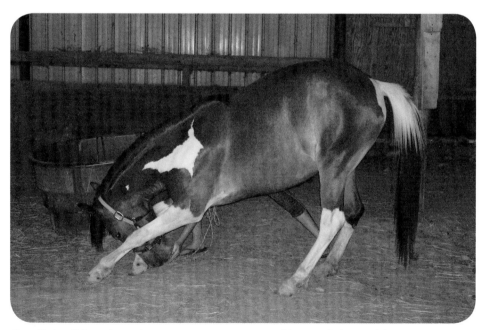

Starlight Blessing demonstrates one of her tricks: taking a bow. Chincoteague ponies are very intelligent and highly trainable.

Summer Barrick rides Sea Feather. Chincoteague ponies are no different from other ponies: They need regular care and exercise.

Riding your pony is a terrific way to exercise it. If your pony is sweaty following exercise, you must walk it until it's cool, sponge it down, and dry it.

No matter how well you train your pony, it may still behave in ways you don't expect. It might jump or run if it hears a strange noise. It could rear if it is stung by a bee. It might even buck you off, just because it is feeling sassy. If you ride a lot, the chances are good that you will fall off at least once. That's why you must wear a helmet with a strap every time you ride.

funFACTS

Each year about 10 foals are bought by charities or schools that let their sponsored ponies swim back to Assateague. Maybe your school class or pony club would like to sponsor a Chincoteague pony.

A full-grown pony weighs around 800 pounds, so wear boots to protect your toes in case they're stepped on. Your boots must have heels to keep them from slipping through the saddle's stirrups, too.

It's a lot of work to care for a pony. When you set out on your first ride, the joy you feel will make it worthwhile.

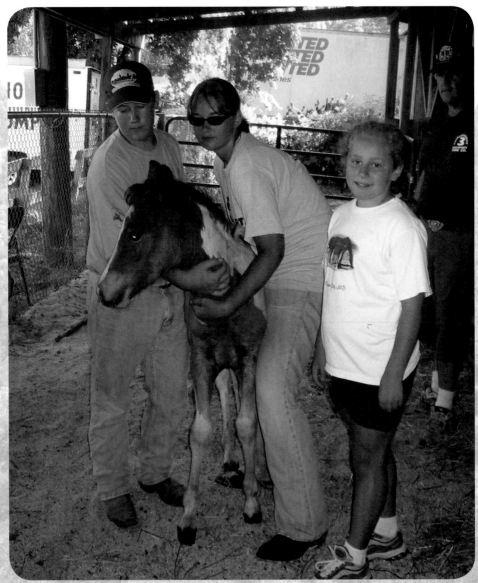

Skylar Hull, right, was excited to get her new foal, Nevaeh's Angel, at the 2007 Chincoteague Pony Auction. Buying and caring for the pony requires the support of her entire family.

Chapter Five

5

ARE YOU READY FOR A WILD PONY?

Wild ponies are beautiful and spirited, but owning one isn't for everyone. Buying a Chincoteague pony often costs thousands of dollars, and that's just the beginning.

You'll have to buy feed, bedding, and grooming supplies. You will need a bridle, saddle, halter, lead rope, blanket, and other equipment. You will have to pay the farrier and the veterinarian. You may need to pay for lessons or entry fees into shows. If you live in the city, you will have to rent pasture and stable space. That can be very expensive.

All these costs add up. The American Horse Council reports that the average cost of caring for a horse is about $3,000 per year. Many people end up spending more. Owning and caring for a wild pony takes a lot of time, energy, and money.

Kailyn Hull, left, hugs her foal, Channing, while her sister, Skylar, leans on her foal, Nevaeh's Angel. Owners say Chincoteague ponies have sweet dispositions.

Many horse owners have to give up new clothes or fun vacations because their horse needs medical care. Are you willing to give up something so that you can help pay for a wild pony instead?

Owning a wild pony is a huge responsibility. Ask yourself if you are ready to care for a pony. Be honest. Will you continue to love your pet for many years to come? Will you clean out its stall every day, and feed it every morning and every night? Will you groom it and give it enough exercise?

It's understandable if your parents are nervous about getting a wild pony. If you're serious about wanting one, you should talk to them about their concerns. You've learned a lot about wild ponies in this book. Share some of the facts you've learned with them. Show them how responsible you are by taking on extra household chores.

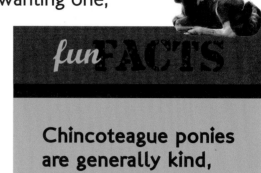

Even if you and your parents decide owning a wild pony is out of the question, you shouldn't give up hope. Maybe you could attend horse camp or volunteer with a riding therapy group. Maybe you could take riding lessons at a local stable.

Another option to explore is horse leasing or renting. If you lease a pony, you will be able to experience the joys and responsibilities of owning a pony without actually having to buy one.

If you and your family decide you are ready to care for a wild pony, you must continue to do your homework. Read everything you can find about wild

Treasured Diamond nuzzles its owner, Elizabeth Suddreth. The two enjoy the time they spend together.

ponies, and begin gathering the supplies you'll need to care for your pet.

The wild ponies of Chincoteague are proud, strong animals. If you are lucky enough to buy and care for a wild pony, you will find you have a pet that brings you years of joy, fun, and faithful companionship.

Books and Articles

Arnosky, Jim. *Wild Ponies: A One Whole Day Book.* New York: National Geographic Children's Books, 2002.

Henry, Marguerite. *Misty of Chincoteague.* New York: Aladdin, revised anniversary edition, 2006; originally published by Rand McNally in 1947.

Henry, Marguerite. *Mustang: Wild Spirit of the West.* New York: Aladdin, 2001.

Jauck, Andrea, and Larry Points. *Assateague: Island of the Wild Ponies.* Mariposa, California: Sierra Press, 2007.

Ransford, Sandy. *The Kingfisher Illustrated Horse and Pony Encyclopedia.* New York: Kingfisher Books, 2004.

Works Consulted

Jauck, Andrea, and Larry Points. *Assateague: Island of the Wild Ponies.* Mariposa, California: Tellurian Press, 1997.

Moore, Kevin N. *The Islands of Assateague & Chincoteague: A Photographer's View.* Lewes, Delaware: Marketplace Merchandising, 2005.

Moore, Kevin N. *A Portrait of the Wild Ponies of Assateague Island and the Chincoteague Pony Swim.* Lewes, Delaware: Marketplace Merchandising, 2006.

Szymanski, Lois. *Out of the Sea: Today's Chincoteague Pony*. Centreville, Maryland: Cornell Maritime Press, Tidewater Publishers, 2007.

Web Addresses

Assateague Island National Seashore
http://www.assateagueisland.com/
Assateague Island National Seashore—Foster Horse Program, http://www.assateaguewildhorses.org/
Assateague's Wild Horses, National Park Service
http://www.nps.gov/asis/naturescience/horses.htm
Chincoteague Island.net
http://www.chincoteague-island.net
The Chincoteague Pony Farm
http://www.rollingbayfarm.com
The Feather Fund
http://www.featherfund.org
Front Range Equine Rescue
http://www.frontrangeequinerescue.org/relatedlinks.html
United States Pony Clubs
http://www.ponyclub.org
Wild Horse and Burro Adoption Information, Bureau of Land Management
https://www.blm.gov/adoptahorse/index.php
Wild Horses of North Carolina's Shackleford Banks
http://www.shacklefordhorses.org

descendants (dee-SEN-dents)—One coming directly from an earlier and usually similar living thing.

farrier (FAA-ree-ur)—A person who is trained to care for horses' hooves.

foals (FOHLS)—Horses or ponies one year old or younger; a male foal is a colt and a female foal is a filly.

galleon (GAL-ee-on)—A large sailing ship.

manure (meh-NOOR)—Animal waste.

mares (MAYRS)—Female horses or ponies.

registered (REH-jis-terd)—Having official papers recorded by a group of breeders.

stallion (STAAL-yen)—A male horse or pony.

trotting (TRAH-ting)—Going faster than a walk and slower than a canter or a gallop.

veterinarian (veh-truh-NAYR-ee-un)—A doctor who cares for animals.

INDEX

Northport-East Northport Public Library

To view your patron record from a computer, click on
the Library's homepage: **www.nenpl.org**

You may:
- request an item be placed on hold
- renew an item that is overdue
- view titles and due dates checked out on your card
- view your own outstanding fines

151 Laurel Avenue
Northport, NY 11768
631-261-6930